BOTANICALS

Adult Coloring Book

Calming Art Therapy

For Encouragement and Self-Love

Evie Vincent Publishing

This Book Belongs To

Thank You

Thank you so much for choosing our botanical coloring book! Your support means the world to us, and we're genuinely grateful for your purchase.

Follow us on Facebook and Instagram and visit us directly at www.EvieVincentPublishing to join our exclusive members-only offerings.

Thank you again for your support, and we hope you continue to find joy and relaxation within the pages of our coloring books.

With Gratitude,
Evie Vincent Publishing

Inspiring

Resilient

Captivating

Brave

Loving

Hard-Working

Motivated

Deserving

Connected

Uplifting

Graceful

Caring

Thoughtful

Blessed

Brilliant

Giving

Reliable

Intelligent

Gorgeous

Authentic

Generous

Capable

Sensible

Charming

Faithful

Hopeful

Compassionate

Courageous

Gracious

Extraordinary

Be Uniquely You

We hope you enjoyed this Botanical collection and look forward to our next offerings.

Stay true to yourself and live abundantly.

Evie Vincent Publishing

Made in United States
Troutdale, OR
02/04/2024